P9-EJI-155

COMBATTING SHAMING
and Toxic Communities™

COMBATTING INTERNET SHAMING

TRACY BROWN HAMILTON

ROSEN PUBLISHING®
New York

Published in 2017 by The Rosen Publishing Group, Inc.
29 East 21st Street, New York, NY 10010

First Edition

Library of Congress Cataloging-in-Publication Data

Names: Hamilton, Tracy Brown, editor.
Title: Combatting internet shaming / Tracy Brown Hamilton.
Description: New York : Rosen Publishing, 2017. | Series: Combatting shaming and toxic communities | Audience: Grades 7-12. | Includes bibliographical references and index.
Identifiers: LCCN 2015045893 | ISBN 9781508171164 (library bound)
Subjects: LCSH: Shame—Juvenile literature. | Internet—Moral and ethical aspects—Juvenile literature.
Classification: LCC BF575.S45 H36 2016 | DDC 302.33—dc23
LC record available at http://lccn.loc.gov/2015045893

Manufactured in China

CONTENTS

INTRODUCTION

Have you ever felt shame? How did it feel? What did you do to make it go away? Shame is a complicated emotion. On one hand, according to a Chinese proverb, shame is a good thing because it is "the beginning of integrity." This suggests that, if you can identify and understand shame, it can help you do the right thing.

But shame is also destructive. It is closely associated with, but different from, guilt. When you feel guilt you feel bad about something you've done. Your actions, more than your character, make you feel bad. But, according to psychoanalyst Helen B. Lewis, feeling shame means feeling bad about *yourself*, feeling you are not a good person.

Sometimes, we shame others as a way to punish them. In fact, in some very recent cases, judges have come up with punishment for criminals that is specifically designed to make someone who has broken the law have to face the public and own up to a behavior considered unacceptable.

For example, a ferry operator in Massachusetts was found guilty of polluting. He received a substantial fine. But the judge also ordered his employer to publish an advertisement in the *Boston Herald* reading: "Our company has discharged human waste directly into coastal Massachusetts waters." This was intended to shame the company and surely had a longer-lasting effect than the fine did.

The Internet is a wonderful resource, but it also can be dangerous. It has made it easy to inflict harm on others by shaming them in a way that is far-reaching and permanent.

Shaming others to change their behavior is not new, but the Internet and social media have opened the gates for people to shame others—be it a stranger or ex-partner or a corporation—on a large scale, reaching thousands of viewers with the likes of tweets, Facebook posts, and online comments.

Targets can now be shamed online with a distribution speed that never existed before, reaching an audience that the person doing the shaming didn't necessarily intend. For example, if someone takes a photo of a stranger and posts it to his or her Twitter account that has only forty followers, it can be picked up and retweeted thousands and thousands of times, expanding the reach of the shaming.

As such shaming messages spread over the Internet, they create a bandwagon effect, in which others are compelled to join in on the shaming and sharing, and with increased intensity. The consequences—in some cases, losing a job, breaking up a relationship, even suicide—often are greater than the original perceived offense.

This resource examines what Internet shaming is, why people do it, and why, in the end, it's a dangerous practice. The Internet is a wonderful place, but it can also be vicious and harmful. Internet shaming is just one of the ways people show their uglier sides online, to tragic and unfair consequences.

WHAT IS INTERNET SHAMING?

Have you ever had attention put on you that you didn't really want? Maybe you tripped and fell on the school bus and wished nobody had seen you fall. How did people react? Did they laugh at you, or did they ask if you were OK? How did you feel?

We live in a world of blurred lines between what is reality and what is entertainment, what is private and what is for public consumption. From reality television programs that give us glimpses at the personal conversations and actions that go on behind closed doors to social media celebrities who gain enormous followings, the Internet and social media have fueled our desire to gossip, gawk, and intrude.

Some people want this attention online, actively seeking it out or accepting it as part of being famous. But for others who become known online, the focus on them is unwelcome, often hurtful. And the ways in which the Internet public responds to the people they read about or see online has become increasingly hostile.

Internet shaming is the act of distributing information, be it a message or a photo or video, about a particular target online

Many teens are inspired by the constant social media presence of celebrities like Kim Kardashian. As we share more of ourselves online, we risk exposure to the wrong elements.

with the intent to cause reputation damage. It is a practice that has grown as social media expands and makes the world an ever-smaller place. Technology has increased our ability to share and connect with each other, but it has also given us new tools for tormenting and causing others pain.

Internet Shaming vs. Online Bullying

Both Internet shaming and online bullying are uses of social media and the Internet that carry bad consequences. But although both practices involve distributing content about a person with the intention to cause harm, online bullying and Internet shaming are not exactly the same.

With online bullying, technology is used to make fun of or even frighten someone. Maybe someone spreads rumors about another person on Facebook or shares unflattering photos with the intention to mock another person for his or her appearance. Online or cyberbullying has the same intentions as regular bullying—to humiliate or intimidate a person—only online you can do so with a far greater audience, around the clock.

Internet shaming usually occurs when someone thinks a target—a business or an individual—deserves to be punished

Because taking and sharing photos has become so easy, people have begun shaming others for their public behavior online. This man was photographed for the "shameful" practice of manspreading.

for something he or she has done that is unacceptable socially. Sometimes, what is at stake may appear small. For example, a recent online photo campaign aimed to end the practice of what has become known as manspreading—men who take up too much room on public trains by sitting with their legs spread out too far. It has become very popular to share photos of men doing this on Twitter (#manspreading) with the intention of shaming these men into being more considerate of other passengers.

But other times, Internet shaming can cause unwarranted—and even unintended—harm to others. People who bully online intend to cause humiliation to their victims. People who shame people online often intend the same—but sometimes, the punishment that results is greater than anticipated or desired.

Why Internet Shaming Is So Dangerous

Even when a person is sure his or her target deserves some degree of punishment, Internet shaming is dangerous because its outcome is never predictable. Anything that is published online is fair game and takes on a life of its own. It is impossible to limit the times or platforms on which content is shared, perceived, or used.

Even if you think your social media reach is limited—perhaps you have just a few Facebook friends or a handful of Twitter followers—you can never be sure where your posts will end up. This is true for what you post about yourself or what others post about you.

For example, in 2013 public relations executive Justine Sacco was preparing to board an airplane to South Africa, and she tweeted this message: "Going to Africa. Hope I don't get AIDS. Just kidding. I'm White!" Sacco didn't have many Twitter followers, and she claims she'd intended this as a joke, as a mockery of what an actual racist person would think about AIDS being an "African" thing. She thought her followers, who knew her, would understand her sarcasm.

But while she was in the air and offline, the tweet was picked up and shared by an editor at Gawker.com, and it quickly had thousands of shares. Sacco became the target of Internet scorn and quickly lost her job. Her reputation and career were destroyed.

The editor who shared the tweet later apologized, saying he hadn't understood the consequences it would have for Sacco, whom he later met and now says was wronged. "Not knowing anything about her," he wrote in a 2014 column on Gawker, "I had taken [her tweet's] cluelessness at face value, and hundreds of thousands of people had done the same—instantly hating her because it's easy and thrilling to hate a stranger online."

MONICA LEWINSKY ON "THE PRICE OF SHAME"

When she was twenty-four years old, Monica Lewinsky found herself the focus of a political scandal after it was revealed that she'd had an affair with then US president Bill Clinton. This was in 1998, and although the incident predates the social media sites millions access today, her

(continued on the next page)

(continued from the previous page)

story was one of the first to nearly, as we say, break the Internet. It was a new age of round-the-clock, round-the-world online media frenzies, and Lewinsky became a household name. She was ridiculed, despised, and shamed by millions around the world.

Nearly twenty years later, Lewinsky delivered a 2015 TED Talk that addressed what she calls a "culture of humiliation." She recalls how, overnight, she "went from being a completely private figure to a publicly humiliated one worldwide. I was patient zero of losing a personal reputation on a global scale almost instantaneously." Lewinsky lost her reputation and her dignity, which was a high price to pay for one mistake—albeit a big mistake.

Monica Lewinsky became a household name for all the wrong reasons before the time of social media. She now works to educate people about the dangers of public shaming.

"Cruelty to others is nothing new," Lewinsky says. "But online, technologically enhanced shaming is amplified, uncontained, and permanently accessible. The echo of embarrassment used to extend only as far as your family, village, school or community, but now it's the online community too. Millions of people, often anonymously, can stab you with their words, and that's a lot of pain, and there are no perimeters around how many people can publicly observe you and put you in a public stockade. There is a very personal price to public humiliation, and the growth of the Internet has jacked up that price."

Lewinsky says we need a shift in how we behave online. "We need to return to a long-held value of compassion—compassion and empathy. Online, we've got a compassion deficit, an empathy crisis." The price of not making this shift is too high and too common, and Lewinsky urges everyone to be more kind online.

Think Twice Before Shaming

Shaming others has become one of the most common uses of the Internet. It can destroy people's lives and reputations. We live in a free-speech society where everyone has a voice. We can express our disapproval for actions we feel are unjust or unethical, but too often with Internet shaming the consequences of bad behavior can be out of balance with the actual "crime" committed.

A person making a bad joke in private company can recover more quickly because the person has a smaller audience and

Incidents of shaming and bullying through the Internet are so pervasive and so harmful that the federal government has set up an initiative to combat the practice on their website at Stopbullying.gov.

because it's less likely that the comment could be taken far out of context. When posting anything on social media, take into account how it might be received by people who don't know you or the subject of your post, and consider what damage the post could potentially cause.

As journalist Laura Hudson wrote in *Wired* magazine, "At its best, social media has given a voice to the disenfranchised, allowing them to bypass the gatekeepers of power and publicize injustices that might otherwise remain invisible. At its worst, it's a weapon of mass reputation destruction, capable of amplifying slander, bullying, and casual idiocy on a scale never before possible."

INTERNET SHAMING AS A FORM OF BULLYING

Sometimes Internet shaming is done as a matter of social vigilantism—when a person decides to react to what he or she perceives as bad behavior by embarrassing the culprit online—but other times, it is a deliberate form of bullying.

Internet shaming for the sake of bullying is almost always a response to a prejudice or bias a person has, something that person wants to strike out against. Sites that show photographs of people shopping at Walmart, for example, aim to mock people who are considered ridiculous or less worthy than the person posting the photo.

This type of shaming also tends to draw the cruelest of commenters—people who respond by piling on their own shame, often seeming to compete with each other to make the most insensitive comment in the name of fun or free expression.

What exactly is the goal of those people who like to make fun of Walmart shoppers who wear unattractive clothing or bring strange accessories with them?

Shaming People Because They Are Overweight

So-called fat-shaming is a common type of Internet shaming that can be classified as bullying. Caitlin Seida recently dressed up as *Tomb Raider* character Lara Croft and shared her photo on Facebook. The photo made its way to a site that is designed to mock people for how they look.

Logging on to Facebook one day, Seida had a message from a friend, telling her she was "Internet famous." Her photo had gone viral, which initially amused Seida. And then she read the comments.

She shared some of them in an essay on Salon.com: "'What a waste of space,' read one. Another: 'Heifers like her should be put down.' Yet another said I should just kill myself 'and spare everyone's eyes.' Hundreds of hateful messages, most of them

POP SINGER PINK SHAMES HER SHAMERS

Internet shaming can happen to anyone. Pop singer Pink was body shamed online in 2013 after a photo of her appeared on Twitter. Pink, who appeared with her daughter at a cancer benefit, was the target of insensitive and insulting comments about her weight. She responded perfectly, saying she could see that some people were "concerned about her," and went on to say:

"You're referring to the pictures of me from last night's cancer benefit that I attended to support my dear friend Dr. Maggie DiNome. She was given the Duke Award for her tireless efforts and stellar contributions to the eradication of cancer. But unfortunately, my weight seems much more important to some of you. While I admit that the dress didn't photograph as well as it did in my kitchen, I will also admit that I felt very pretty. In fact, I feel beautiful. So, my good and concerned peoples, please don't worry about me. I'm not worried about me. And I'm not worried about you either."

saying that I was a worthless human being and shaming me for having the audacity to go in public dressed as a sexy video game character. How dare I dress up and have a good time!"

More recently, comedian Nicole Arbour posted a YouTube video called "Dear Fat People," in which she tries to convince heavy people to lose weight by making fun of them relentlessly. The video reached three million views but led to Arbour's being fired from a movie she had been hired to work on.

Shaming People Because They Are Gay

Pop singer Justin Bieber has had comments regarding his sexuality spread around the Internet for years—calling him gay, even calling him a lesbian. And in a recent tweet the singer shot back, saying that no, he isn't gay, but even if he was, "gay" is not an insult.

Rutgers students paid their respects to Tyler Clementi after he committed suicide following a shaming incident. Sexual orientation is a common theme of Internet shaming, when actually there's no shame in being gay at all.

Still, many people want to keep quiet about their sexuality, especially if they are confused about it, are just experimenting, or haven't yet come out to friends and family.

What may seem like a prank can have tragic consequences. In 2010, Rutgers University student Tyler Clementi committed suicide after his roommate secretly filmed him kissing another man. This invasion of his sexual privacy directly led to his suicide, after the video was posted on Twitter.

The roommate was charged with a hate crime and later told television news program *20/20* that while he regretted his "dumb kid" actions, he didn't feel responsible for his roommate's death. "Even though I wasn't the one who caused him to jump off the bridge," he said, "I did do things wrong and I was stupid about a lot of stuff."

Surprisingly it's not just young people who engage in this type of gay shaming. Online news source Gawker.com outed the CFO of Condé Nast in 2015, after a young man who had been hired as an escort for him brought the story to an editor (although the arrangement was canceled with the escort and nothing ever happened). Gawker later apologized, but the damage to the CFO, his wife, and his three children was already done.

People who want to bully you will always look for your vulnerable spot, what can hurt you or humiliate you the most. And with the Internet, bullies can cast a much wider, more damaging net.

Other Types of Internet Shaming

There are many ways to torment someone online. There are shaming sites dedicated to people's exes, either showing explicit photos or revealing other private details. In 2015, one

Negative messages, such as those fueled by sexism or racism, have just as destructive an impact online as off. Behaving online just as you would behave in person is a good rule to follow when using the Internet.

so-called revenge porn site was shut down by the United States Federal Trade Commission (FTC), which also banned its operator, Colorado resident Craig Brittain, from sharing any more nude photos or videos of people without their consent.

There are "hate sites" that post content that is racist, sexist, or homophobic. Identity theft online occurs when someone pretends to be someone else, starting with logging on to social media sites as that person and then posting content that misrepresents and damages the person.

This sort of shaming and bullying is every bit as harmful as physical bullying. When you deliberately set out to humiliate someone or ruin his or her reputation, it is never "just a joke."

What Does the Law Say?

With increasing awareness of the damage Internet shaming can cause, what are the legal rights of its victims? It depends on the type of shaming that occurs. Although states like California have made revenge porn illegal, other forms of Internet shaming or bullying are more difficult to criminalize. Trollers—people who leave deliberately scathing or offensive comments online—often do so anonymously and are protected by free speech laws. You can sue for defamation—injury to reputation—but according to the blog FindLaw, "irritating or annoying someone online is often outside of the law's grasp." And according to the site OpposingViews, everything on the Internet is a "gray area." Although making a fake Facebook profile isn't illegal in and of itself, "there are several ways to get yourself in trouble depending on your intent and whom the profile supposedly represents. As a rule of thumb, impersonating other, real people is a bad idea. Making a fake profile for a public official—even an imaginary one, in some states—can also be a serious crime.

INTERNET SHAMING TO CHANGE BEHAVIOR

Does anyone ever deserve to be shamed online? One of the justifications many people use for engaging in Internet shaming is that their target deserves to be publicly punished for a wrongdoing. This type of shaming can be directed at an individual or a corporation that engages in behaviors that are perceived as unethical or socially unacceptable.

The idea behind using the Internet to call "offenders" out on their behavior is to first punish and humiliate the target, but second to discourage others from acting in the same ways. But there is no evidence to support Internet shaming as an effective means of discouraging people or companies from acting badly.

It can be very tempting to use social media and the Internet to shame people—sometimes people you know, like an ex-boyfriend or ex-girlfriend, and often someone you don't. It's so easy to retweet a message, comment on a post, or share a photo on

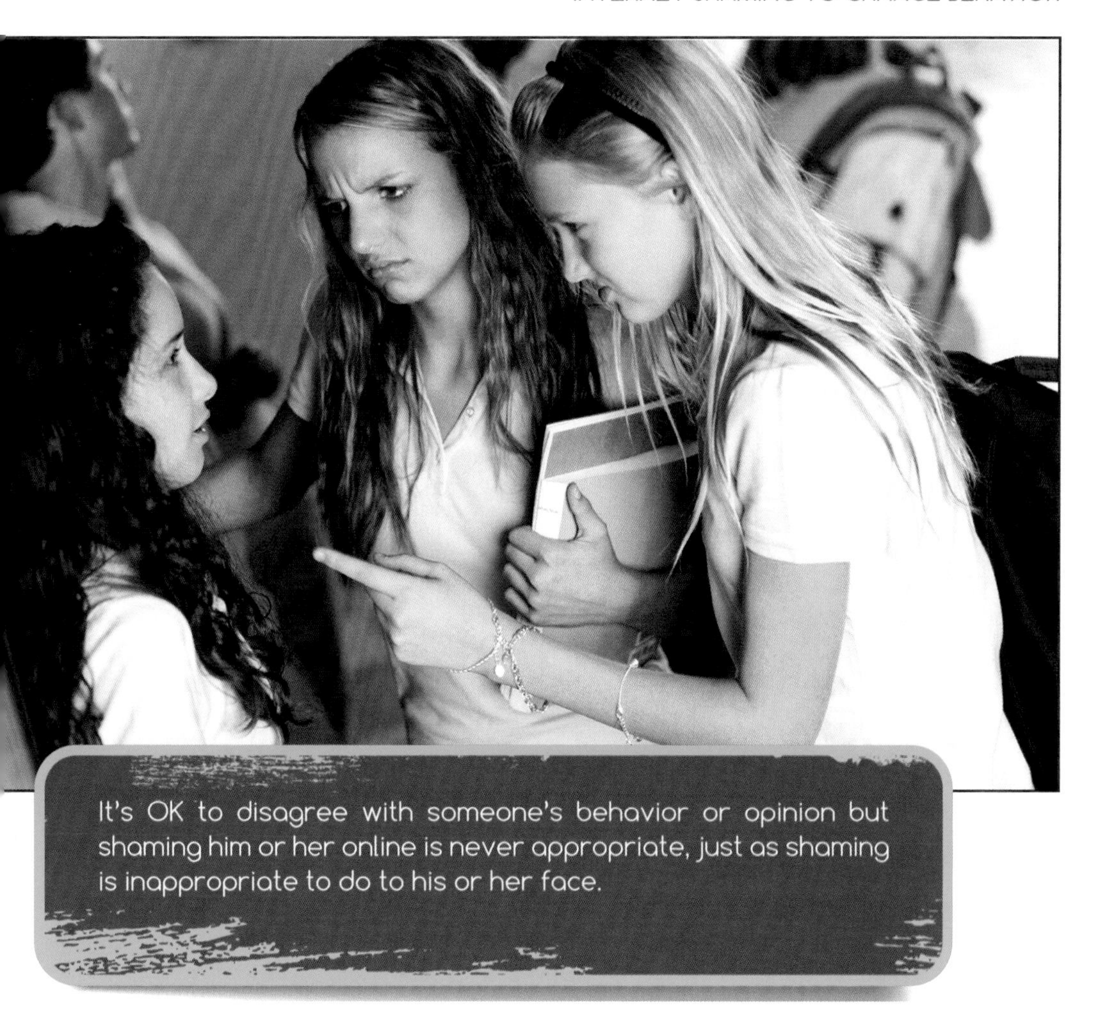

It's OK to disagree with someone's behavior or opinion but shaming him or her online is never appropriate, just as shaming is inappropriate to do to his or her face.

Facebook intending to express disagreement or disapproval. Doing so, however, can lead to unforeseen consequences.

Public Shaming as Mob Justice

Mob justice occurs when a large group of people takes justice into their own hands. In a *New Statesmen* article, writer Tauriq Moosa used an incident about Paris Hilton as an example to illustrate mob justice. After the death of Nelson Mandela, a Twitter account supposedly belonging to Paris Hilton shared a post thanking Mandela for his "I Have a Dream" speech. That speech had actually been delivered by Dr. Martin Luther King Jr.

In no time at all, the tweet made its way around the Internet, and Hilton was mocked by hundreds of people. According to Moosa, "people quickly informed Ms. Hilton that she was all kinds of idiot, all kinds of female anatomy parts, all kinds of waste product." The truth is, we don't know that she actually wrote the tweet. And even if she did, the vulgarity and inappropriateness of the comments thrown at her were incredibly offensive—even if she made the mistake, is that type of response warranted or equal to the wrongdoing?

The problem with mob justice on the Internet is people don't always have their facts straight, and they don't always react appropriately or in a way that fits the "crime." As Moosa writes, "If you think you have moral immunity in how you respond to an act you deem wrong, if you're bolstered by witnessing mutual reaction and views from others to the wrong act, this is essentially *mob justice*."

Unpredictable Outcomes for the Shamer and the Shamed

The Internet is a vast and unpredictable space. The second you post something online, you lose control over where it will go and how it will be received. Sometimes, the consequences are far greater than intended.

Such was the case with Adria Richards, a woman who attended the PyCon tech conference as part of her job. During the conference, Richards overheard two men making jokes that she found sexist and offensive (the jokes were about two tech terms, "dongle" and "forking"). In retaliation, Richards photographed the men without them knowing and posted a tweet of the photo along with a complaint: “Not cool. Jokes about ‘forking’ repo’s in a sexual way and big ‘dongles.’” The first result was that one of the men was fired. When this became news, Richards herself became the target of Internet rage, being called sexually offensive names, receiving insinuations that she should be raped and otherwise harmed, and being called a man-hater.

WHEN INTERNET SHAMING LEADS TO DEATH THREATS

Walter Palmer, a dentist from Minnesota, became arguably the most hated man on the Internet when he shot and killed a beloved lion in Zimbabwe while hunting. Although he was not charged with a crime, when his identity was released on the Internet he received death threats and a holiday home of his was vandalized. He was forced to temporarily close his dental practice because of threats by animal rights protesters and other groups. Palmer—despised by thousands around the globe—had to hire security to help himself and his family feel safe.

Taking to the Internet is an easy but dangerous way to vent frustrations. Instead of letting someone know he or she is making you uncomfortable, blasting criticism and "outing" perpetrators online can have exaggerated consequences for everyone involved.

Richards perhaps did not want to see the men get fired but instead wanted to make a point about the existence of sexism in the tech industry. Consequently, a father of three lost his job and Richards became the target of much more aggressive sexual online abuse.

Shaming People into Having Better Manners

Sometimes people are not actually offended but more irritated by the behavior of others. Part of living in a society and sharing public spaces and transportation means having to deal with people who do things that get on your nerves. Maybe someone is sitting next to you on the bus chewing gum very loudly, or maybe someone is talking on the phone during a movie. These behaviors can be annoying or rude, but they are generally not deeply offensive acts.

Still, in an attempt to correct such behavior in public, there are websites that serve to mock and shame people who cross the line. There's a site, for example, that features people behaving badly on airplanes and includes images of passengers putting their feet on the tray tables or not wearing a shirt inflight. This so-called passenger shaming site includes this description: "Are these [expletive] serious? Photos taken by anonymous flight attendants & passengers from all over the world. Don't end up here."

It's a fine line between venting your frustrations and publicizing bad behavior over the Internet. Instead of posting a shaming photo of your fellow passenger, why not ask her to move her seatback forward?

The People of Walmart site makes fun of shoppers that dress, look, or act in ways considered "funny." Although the site includes a disclaimer letting users know to keep it nice, strangers photograph strangers and post their images online without permission nonetheless.

Posting Photos of Strangers Is a Violation of Privacy

In the name of humor or punishment, we seem to have become immune to the gross violation of privacy it is to post photos of other people online without receiving their permission. With so many people carrying around smartphones or tablets, it's very easy to snap a photo in a public place and post it online—but that doesn't mean we should, even if the law says it's not a crime.

For example, in 2014 the Supreme Judicial Court of Massachusetts tossed out charges against a Boston subway rider who was caught taking photos up the skirts of female

People who are innocently walking around in public should not expect to have their photos taken by strangers and posted online. But with the prevalence of smartphones, this has become common practice.

subway users. The decision was made because the law that was being used to prosecute the man only applied to "partially nude" women in a private place: "A female passenger on a MBTA trolley who is wearing a skirt, dress, or the like covering these parts of her body is not a person who is 'partially nude,' no matter what is or is not underneath the skirt by way of underwear or other clothing . . . [B]ecause the MBTA is a public transit system operating in a public place and uses cameras, the two alleged victims here were not in a place and circumstance where they reasonably would or could have had an expectation of privacy."

If you are in a public place, it's true that you can't have an expectation of privacy. But being in public does not mean the same things as being online, where photos become memes, and where people post with the intent to shame subjects they know nothing about.

WHEN INTERNET SHAMING BACKFIRES

Adam Smith, former CFO and treasurer of medical supplies manufacturer Vante, attempted to shame a fast food worker because the president and COO of her employer, Chick-fil-A, spoke out against gay marriage.

After ordering water from the drive-through, Smith told the employee, "I don't know how you live with yourself and work here." He continued, "I don't understand it. This is a horrible corporation with horrible values. You deserve better. [. . .] I'm a nice guy, by the way . . . totally heterosexual . . . I just can't stand the hate."

Smith videotaped the incident and posted it on YouTube. His verbal attack of the Chick-fil-A worker got angry responses, and Smith was promptly fired. Reportedly, he was let go from a subsequent job after his new employer learned about the incident, and Smith and his family were forced to live in a trailer and collect food stamps.

Does Shaming to Change Behavior Even Work?

Experts say that this type of shaming is actually not effective in correcting how people act in public and that it does more harm than good. In a recent example, a man sent a photo of his private parts to a woman on a dating site, who promptly sent it to the man's mother. Many thought he deserved this, but others felt it was going too far. In another case, a woman overheard a man on a train bragging about cheating on his wife. She posted a photo of him on Facebook asking, "Is this your husband?" It was shared thousands of times.

But does either example put an end to infidelity or unwanted, crass photo sharing? Do men still take up too much space on the subway? Have passengers improved their manners on airplanes? Experts say there is no evidence to support that Internet shaming changes people's behavior. If anything, it has only created a toxic environment online.

WHEN PARENTS SHAME THEIR CHILDREN

We've talked about bullies and would-be vigilantes who shame people online. But Internet shaming is a practice that parents are increasingly doing to their own children, as a means of what some call creative discipline. These unconventional punishments take advantage of technology to ensure the child is not only reprimanded but humiliated on a broad scale. The idea is that if parents sufficiently embarrass children for a particular behavior, that behavior will not be repeated. But many experts denounce the practice as ineffective and even abusive.

There have been many forms of parents shaming their children. There was the father who posted a video of himself shooting his daughter's laptop and the mother who gave her misbehaving son an "old-man" haircut as punishment. The Internet sometimes responds gleefully to these posts, but more recently these techniques have been criticized as harmful to children, if not deadly.

Parents who punish their children by humiliating them online are, according to some research, doing way more harm than good. It's the equivalent of being made to wear a dunce cap.

How Parents Shame Their Children

One common method of humiliation as punishment is parents who force their children to stand on street corners wearing signs that announce their crimes: "I drank beer," "I stole money," "I skipped school." Often photos of children being punished are later shared online.

One mother in Australia sold her daughter's concert tickets on eBay—in itself, not abusive, but she included in the listing a long message to her daughter that began: "You can thank my daughters self righteous and lippy attitude for their sale. See sweety? And you thought I was bluffing. I hope the scowl on your [expletive] little friends faces when you tell them that your dad and i revoked the gift we were giving you all reminds you that your PARENTS are the ones that deserve love and respect more than anyone."

Parents can get caught up in the struggle to raise their children. But what may feel like a harmless joke or an effective strategy to some parents may actually be harming their children.

And it doesn't just happen to teenagers. One father shamed his three-year-old daughter for accidently defecating in the shower. He posted a photo of her standing facing the camera in her pajamas, a sign around her neck reading: "I pooped in the shower and daddy had to clean it up. I hereby sign this as permission to use in my yearbook senior year."

When his actions led to outrage online, he defended his choice, telling the *Daily Mail* that he "personally thought it was funny and wasn't looking for attention but merely trying to give parents that are able to laugh at these silly things a chance to." He signed a paper giving his daughter permission to do the same thing to him when he's "old and decrepit."

"I'D NEVER EMBARRASS MY KID LIKE THAT"

Florida dad Wayman Gresham posted a Facebook video in 2015 that at first appeared to be yet another example of shame discipline. In the video, he stands next to his son, who is sitting in a chair. Gresham tells the camera he is going to teach his son a lesson and then says, "I don't teach him to mess up in school, I don't teach him to be a fool." He seems about to shave his son's head, but instead asks him for a hug and lets him go.

Gresham then talks about the role of parents and how public shaming doesn't help. "There's no way in the world I would ever embarrass my son like that," he says. "Good parenting starts before he even gets to the point of being out of control."

He finds the trend really disturbing. "I've gone on Facebook and many times I've seen this kind of punishment, cutting of the hair or a child being embarrassed one way or another," Gresham said, according to BBC Trending. "There is no legitimate reason for humiliating your child, there is no legitimate reason for snatching their dignity."

Shaming Doesn't Teach Lessons

Shaming someone is certainly punishment, but is it an effective way for parents to guide their children to behave sensibly, responsibly, and honestly? Most experts will say that shaming children does nothing enriching, but instead serves to damage self-worth.

Dr. Gail Gross, Ph.D., Ed.D., M.Ed, says it's never OK for parents to shame a child. As she told Parenting.com, "A parent that shames their child is violating all the basic [tenets] of what parenting is about. Parents are supposed to be their safety net."

Online shaming is not an effective punishment tool. In addition, it is difficult to recover from because the Internet allows for a wider audience and a longer life span of any comment or photo.

She adds that the effects of shaming can be permanent. "Shaming children violates their trust in their parents and can lead to permanent, lifelong problems for kids. Every relationship is based on early childhood patterns," she says.

According to Gross, shaming impacts the development of a child, creating undue stress and affecting the brain. Anxiety and depression can result later in life, and some kids suffer post-traumatic stress disorder after being shamed by a parent. Some have even committed suicide.

Embarrassing Children to Death

More than an exaggeration, shaming children as punishment—whether a peer or a parent or a stranger is the culprit—can lead to tragic consequences. In 2015, a thirteen-year-old girl jumped off a bridge to her death after her father cut off her hair as punishment.

Izabel Laxamana committed suicide just days after her dad, Jeff, videotaped the hair-cutting incident. In the video, a male voice can be heard saying, "The consequences of getting messed up, man, you lost all that beautiful hair." He asks her: "Was it worth it?" What she was in trouble for is not clear.

The video appeared online, although the father says he didn't post it. It is believed by many to have played a part in her killing herself. A Facebook page called "Justice For Izabel" decries her father's actions and those of other parents who engage in similar punishment tactics with their children.

HOW WE CAN PREVENT INTERNET SHAMING

The Internet is a powerful tool used daily by millions to communicate, work, learn, and be entertained. However, it has also become an unfriendly and aggressive place where trollers post caustic comments to start arguments and people—often in large groups—punish and humiliate targets they feel deserve it.

There are some laws that can be applied to online behavior, but they were drafted to be used in real-world, offline circumstances. Defamation, intentional infliction of emotional distress, and impersonation are all crimes, but lawmakers have been uncertain how to translate these to the relatively new problem of Internet shaming and bullying. Until we can look to the law to prevent Internet shaming, we need to find other means of improving our behavior online.

People are meaner online than they might be in person because it's safer. It's anonymous, for one, and for some—like trollers, who deliberately post negative comments to incite

Because social media is relatively new, legislators have been a little slow to create laws that protect people from Internet shaming.

arguments—it's a form of entertainment. People who might otherwise feel powerless feel enormously important. People who are otherwise shy can become aggressive. The Internet and social media have given people a means to be their darkest selves. But is this something we just have to accept, or is there something we can do about it?

Having More Empathy Online

Empathy means being able to experience and relate to the emotions of another person. People with empathy feel bad if they

The anonymity of online commenting and posting has perhaps made people less empathic, which is an important characteristic to develop for a healthy, functioning society.

make someone cry because they can identify crying as something you do when you feel hurt or sad. Empathy keeps us from hurting one another and from enjoying the pain we see others experiencing.

One easy way to prevent the spread of Internet shaming is to personally stop sharing and spreading content online that aims to humiliate or harm. It is psychologically easier to dehumanize someone you see online whom you do not know and who is being presented in a negative or funny context, but behind these viral videos are actual people, with parents, siblings, maybe children of their own. You probably would not laugh at these people to their face, so you shouldn't do it online.

"Empathy means to really connect with and understand another person's situation, feelings, or difficulties," says blogger Jeff Roberts. "Putting yourself in this space will fill you with a genuine compassion that will help you gain a true understanding of the matter at hand. It is a brave space to put yourself in, allowing yourself to identify and feel a feeling that may not always be good. But if we all practiced bringing more empathy into our lives, the world would be a much better place for it."

What Social Media Companies Can Do

Even if the law can't monitor human behavior online, companies that provide the forum for social media interactions can keep an eye on how their users behave. In 2015, Reddit—a social media, entertainment, and news site with an interactive community that can post and respond to content—recently announced it is "unhappy with harassing behavior." Defining harassment as "systematic and/or continued actions to torment or demean someone," the company said users who are being harassed should report it. Reddit will review each complaint and ban users it determines have been abusive. The site also promises to remove images, videos, or links to explicit content if published without the permission of the subject.

Facebook has also improved its prevention measures against online abuse by making it easy for users to report posts or other content that they find offensive. Sites like Facebook and Twitter have also made it easier to control who can view your content and who can share information with you through various security settings.

TIPS FOR PROTECTING YOURSELF FROM INTERNET SHAMING

Just because the world is now crawling with smartphones equipped with cameras and WiFi doesn't mean you have to go around acting on your best behavior just in case you are being photographed. But there are ways you can protect yourself from being embarrassed online.

- Always log out of social media sites when you are done.
- Never leave your accounts open for anyone to access and abuse.
- Never photograph yourself or allow yourself to be photographed in any way that could be misconstrued or embarrassing in the wrong hands or context.
- Don't be a bully yourself. Post content that encourages compassion rather than retaliation. Don't engage with trollers.
- Set your privacy controls on all devices and never reveal your passwords to anyone.

Protect Yourself: Be Careful What You Post

As several examples in this book illustrate, Internet shaming is often brought on by something the "shamed" parties posted themselves. Remember that your comments—which to you may be funny or just isolated rants—can spread wide and far, and they can become misinterpreted and offensive. Don't let yourself be the target of mass Internet disdain because of a careless post.

Even if you later delete a tweet or Facebook post, you never know where it's already spread. Reputations, jobs, friends, and even lives have been lost over online content that has spiraled out of control. Remember that anything you put online will take on a life of its own and can never be truly erased. Think twice and ask yourself how someone who doesn't know you may interpret your message or whether someone could inadvertently get his or her feelings or reputation hurt by it.

Don't Do Online What You'd Never Do Offline

Do you think you act with the same manners and morals online as you do in your real life? Are you just as polite, respectful, and kind? Imagine you are sitting on an airplane and a couple sitting next to you is in the middle of a breakup. The woman is clearly upset—she's crying, she pleading, she's sharing personal information. It is happening in public, but it is still a private moment. Even though you might be able to hear it, you would probably not stand up and repeat everything to the people at the other

Your online behavior should mimic how you would treat people and represent yourself in real life. In addition, you should be as thoughtful about how you communicate online as you are in person.

end of the plane who cannot hear it from where they are sitting.

A woman named Kelly Keegs was in this situation, but instead of yelling to the back of the plane, she began live-tweeting the incident—which *US* magazine called "hilarious." Keegs began by posting: "This guy on the plane just broke up w his girlfriend and she's SOBBING," along with a photo of the woman crying. Keegs went on to tweet more quotes from the heated and very personal conversation ("Guy: 'You need to calm down' Girl: 'To me I just really thought, you know, this was going to go somewhere'"), which was followed by thousands of readers.

In the end, the couple made up. But all the while, they had no idea that they had become the subject of online amusement. Remember that just because something is happening in public, that does not mean it should be happening around the globe without the knowledge of the parties involved.

HOW TO RESPOND TO INTERNET SHAMING

Being shamed online or witnessing the shame of someone else can be uncomfortable and hurtful. It can also be infuriating. How should you react if someone is purposefully trying to damage your reputation on the Internet or punish you for a mistake that you have made?

The worst thing you can do is respond in a way that brings more attention to the situation or gives more power to the person trying to shame you. But there are ways you can keep things from getting worse and ways to turn a shaming incident into something empowering.

Never Engage with a Bully

Not responding is usually good advice in any kind of bullying situation. Most bullies do it for the attention and the response

As difficult as it may be, sometimes the best defense is no defense. Responding to online shamers often just makes the problem worse. Ignoring them can bring faster resolution to the problem.

they can get, and if you don't give that to them, they will stop or move on to another victim.

A problem with engaging in a dialogue with a bully or troller is it tends to escalate rather than calm the situation. Most people who leave scathing remarks in a comments section or post something aggressive or offensive are not going to change their minds because of a rational explanation you may offer. And certainly if you respond in anger, the exchange will not end well.

Psychology Today recently published findings of a Canadian study that looked at what types of people ignite arguments online. They found so-called Internet trolls are "everyday sadists," people who enjoy making you feel bad. So don't let them—ignore them.

THE HIGH PRICE OF SHAME

Even when someone—maybe the CEO of a company or an unfaithful husband—does something we think deserves punishing, shame is a high price to make someone pay. In her TED Talk "The High Price of Shame," researcher and author Brené Brown explains why shaming someone is so detrimental. "The thing to understand about shame is, it's not guilt. Shame is a focus on self, guilt is a focus on behavior. Shame is 'I am bad.' Guilt is 'I did something bad.' How many of you, if you did something that was hurtful to me, would be willing to say, 'I'm sorry. I made a mistake'? How many of you would be willing to say that? Guilt: I'm sorry. I made a mistake. Shame: I'm sorry. I am a mistake.

"There's a huge difference between shame and guilt. And here's what you need to know. Shame is highly, highly correlated with addiction, depression, violence, aggression, bullying, suicide, eating disorders. And here's what you even need to know more. Guilt, inversely correlated with those things. The ability to hold something we've done or failed to do up against who we want to be is incredibly adaptive. It's uncomfortable, but it's adaptive."

React Offensively, Not Defensively

Others have found a way to respond to Internet shaming in a way that turns the spotlight away from the person being shamed and onto the greater issue at stake. When pop singer Ariana Grande was body-shamed on Twitter—another user called her a "stick" and said that curves were more beautiful—she responded not defensively but by attacking head-on the idea that anyone has a right to comment on anyone else's body.

"We live in a day and age where people make it IMPOSSIBLE for women, men, anyone to embrace themselves exactly how they are," Grande wrote. "Diversity is sexy! Loving yourself is sexy! You know what is NOT sexy? Misogyny, objectifying, labeling, comparing and body shaming!!!" What Grande did was take the conversation away from her body and the individual insulting her for it and made it more about something positive: how we should stop shaming each other for our body types and embrace our differences.

Report Instances of Internet Shaming

If you see content that is harmful or derogatory to you or someone else, report it. You can let your Internet service provider or the social media platform on which the content appears know.

The Internet can be a particularly vulnerable place for young adults and children. Let your parents, teacher, or another adult know if someone—a stranger or otherwise—ever makes you a target online.

If someone you know is being shamed over the Internet, do something about it. Show empathy and kindness. Turn the conversation to something positive. And, if necessary, report the shamer.

Respond to Negative Comments with Positive Messages

Anyone can be the victim of Internet shaming, even the successful and famous. Celebrities are not spared the wrath of trollers or Internet shamers, and many have delivered perfect responses to online abusers. When actress Gabourey Sidibe was mocked for her appearance at the Golden Globes, she shut down critics with one fantastic tweet: "To the people making mean comments about my pics, I mos def cried about it on that private jet on the way to my dream job."

RESPONDING TO SLUT SHAMING

When her friend was shamed online in a sexual context—so-called slut shaming—Paloma Brierley Newton did not take it lightly. She posted the following, also revealing the identity of the man who had shamed her friend:

"I want to take a moment to talk about sexual violence and harassment. Today a friend of mine became aware that someone had screen shotted her tinder profile picture and uploaded it onto their Facebook, essentially slut shaming my friend for using lyrics from a song as her tag line. The comments started to get pretty intense and at one point people starting insinuating that my friend should be raped because of her tinder profile. She uploaded the photo and the comments to shame him for his behaviour of harassment and violence against women. This kind of behaviour is what we call 'normalisation of violence against women' and it is really really scary and damaging, it is the reason that every day our mothers, our sisters and our friends are killed by men, and raped by men. I'm also going to shame this man, who aside from insinuating he is going to rape my mother, is also a great example of how NOT TO TALK TO WOMEN just in case anyone needed a bit of help. I'll also be taking these pictures to the police, be warned men, the Internet is not longer your invisibility cloak. I am coming after you and I will not be stopped."

While shaming your shamer is probably not a good idea—it just continues the cycle of shaming—addressing the problem head-on as Paloma Brierley Newton did can help raise needed awareness about what is and is not OK online or elsewhere.

For as many mean-spirited people that there are online, there are also lots of empathetic, good people, and sometimes it takes shamers to bring out the better sides of our humanity. When the boyfriend of twenty-one-year-old Ashley Stevens was mocked online after photos of the couple at a wedding appeared on Reddit, Stevens gave a wonderful response.

Commenters called her boyfriend "fat and disgusting," among other insults, comments Stevens called shallow and rude. "Let me just tell you, I won the jackpot with Christopher," she wrote on Facebook. "He may not have rock hard abs like the world tells girls to want in a guy, but really, why does that even matter when you are trying to really find someone to spend the rest of your life with?

"He is so thoughtful and patient, he always shows me how he loves me in little ways, he is my best friend. I love him for who he is and he loves me for who I am. Understanding, loving, and hilarious, which is so rare to find these days!!" She ends with: "God saw the desires of my heart and blessed me with Christopher."

GLOSSARY

ADAPTIVE Changing to enhance survival.

BODY SHAMING Shaming someone for his or her body size or type.

BULLY A person who regularly torments another person.

CYBERBULLY A person who bullies someone using telephone and Internet technology.

DEFAMATION The act of damaging a person's reputation.

FACEBOOK A social media site where people post photos and messages.

GAY SHAMING Shaming someone for his or her sexual orientation.

HARASSMENT To persistently torment or annoy.

INTERNET SHAMING Using social media and the Internet to shame someone.

MEME Humorous or inflammatory image or video that is spread virally via social media.

MISOGYNY Prejudice against women.

PERPETRATOR A person who commits a crime or offense.

REGRET To feel sadness for past actions.

REPUTATION The generally held opinions or beliefs about a person or organization.

REVENGE PORN The publication of explicit content without consent of the subject with the intent to cause harm.

SADIST A person who enjoys causing pain or harm to others.

SHAMING Making someone feel ashamed or humiliated.

SOCIAL MEDIA Sites that allow people to connect and communicate with others online.

SUICIDE The act of ending one's own life.

TARGET A person who is selected as a potential victim.

TROLLER A person who deliberately starts arguments or angers people with abusive comments online.

TWEET A message posted on Twitter.

TWITTER A social networking site in which people post messages of 140 characters or less.

VICTIM A person against whom a crime or offense is done.

VIGILANTE A person who punishes crimes or perceived crimes without legal authority.

FOR MORE INFORMATION

Bullying Canada
471 Smythe Street
P.O. Box 27009
Fredericton, NB
E3B 9M1
Canada
(877) 352-4497
Website: http://www.bullyingcanada.ca
A nonprofit, youth-created organization dedicated to educating and advising on cyberbullying issues across Canada.

Cyber Bullying Prevention
5N426 Meadowview Lane
St Charles, IL 60175
(847) 769-7495
Website: http://www.cyberbullyingprevention.com
Dedicated to raising awareness of cyberbullying and its negative impacts.

It Gets Better
110 S. Fairfax Avenue, Suite A11-71
Los Angeles, CA 90036
Website: http://www.itgetsbetter.org
The It Gets Better Project was created to show young LGBT people the levels of happiness, potential, and positivity their lives will reach—if they can just get through their teen years.

National Children's Advocacy Center
210 Pratt Ave.
Huntsville, AL 35801
(256) 533-5437
Website: http://www.nationalcac.org
The National Children's Advocacy Center models, promotes, and delivers excellence in child abuse response and prevention, including Internet safety.

Stop a Bully
Website: http://www.stopabully.ca
Stop a Bully is a national nonprofit organization and Canada-wide antibullying program that allows any student who is a victim or witness of severe bullying to be able to safely report the details to school officials.

StopBullying.gov
200 Independence Avenue SW
Washington, DC 20201
Website: http://www.stopbullying.gov
StopBullying.gov provides information from various government agencies on what bullying is, what cyberbullying is, who is at risk, and how you can prevent and respond to bullying.

STOP Cyberbullying
Wired Kids, Inc.
PMB 342 4401-A
Connecticut Ave NW
Washington, DC 20008
(201) 463-8663

Website: http://www.stopcyberbullying.org
An organization dedicated to showing children and educators how they can help prevent and take a stand against the practice of cyberbullying.

#StopShamingKids
(844) 279-0118
Website: http://www.teach-through-love.com/stop-shaming-kids.html
This organization aims to establish parameters to prohibit the public shaming of children on the Internet.

Websites

Because of the changing nature of Internet links, Rosen Publishing has developed an online list of websites related to the subject of this book. This site is updated regularly. Please use this link to access this list:
http://www.rosenlinks.com/CSTC/inter

FOR FURTHER READING

Abram, Carolyn. *Facebook For Dummies.* Hoboken, NJ: Wiley, 2012.

Claypoole, Ted. *Protecting Your Internet Identity*. Lanham, MD: Rowman & Littlefield Publishers, 2012.

Farrell, Amy Erdman. *Fat Shame: Stigma and the Fat Body in American Culture.* New York, NY: NYU Press, 2011.

Gordon, Sherri Mabry. *Are You at Risk for Public Shaming?* New York, NY: Enslow Publishing, 2016.

Green, Susan. *Don't Pick on Me: Help for Kids to Stand Up and Deal with Bullies.* Oakland, CA: Instant Help, 2010.

Greenberg, Grant. *Facebook and Privacy: What You Need to Know to Keep Your Privacy Safe.* Amazon Digital Services, 2010.

Hunter, Nick. *Cyber Bullying.* Mankato, MN: Heinemann-Raintree, 2011.

Ivester, Matt. *LOL...OMG! What Every Student Needs to Know About Online Reputation Management, Digital Citizenship, and Cyberbullying.* Seattle, WA: CreateSpace, 2011.

Kowalski, Robin. *Cyberbullying: Bullying in the Digital Age.* Hoboken, NJ: Wiley-Blackwell, 2012.

Redmond, Sylvia. *Fat-Shaming Is the New Bad Word.* Amazon Digital Services, Inc., 2015.

Ronson, Jon. *So You've Been Publicly Shamed.* New York, NY: Riverhead Books, 2015.

Ryan, Peter. *Online Bullying (Teen Mental Health)*. New York, NY: Rosen Publishing Group, 2011.

Tanenbaum, Leora. *I Am Not a Slut: Slut-Shaming in the Age of the Internet.* New York, NY: Harper Perennial, 2015.

Bernstein, Elizabeth. "Guilt Versus Shame: One Is Productive, the Other Isn't, and How to Tell Them Apart." *Wall Street Journal*, November 3, 2014. Retrieved November 25, 2015 (http://www.wsj.com/articles/guilt-versus-shame-one-is-productive-the-other-isnt-and-how-to-tell-them-apart-1415038844).

Burgo, Joseph. "The Difference Between Guilt and Shame." *Psychology Today*, May 30, 2013. Retrieved November 25, 2015 (https://www.psychologytoday.com/blog/shame/201305/the-difference-between-guilt-and-shame).

Corcoran, Kieran. "Girl, 13, Commits Suicide by Jumping from Bridge After Her Dad Recorded Video Cutting Off Her Hair—but Cops Deny It Drove Her to Kill Herself." *Daily Mail Online*, June 5, 2015. Retrieved November 25, 2015 (http://www.dailymail.co.uk/news/article-3111907/Girl-13-commits-suicide-jumping-bridge-video-dad-cutting-hair-punishment-posted-online.html).

Desiderio, Andrew. "Ex-CFO Who Berated Chick-fil-A Worker in Video Now Lives on Food Stamps." Media Ite, March 29, 2015. Retrieved November 25, 2015 (http://www.mediaite.com/tv/ex-cfo-who-berated-chick-fil-a-worker-in-video-now-lives-on-food-stamps).

Diaz, Joseph, and Lauren Effron. "Former CFO on Food Stamps After Controversial Viral Video About Chick-Fil-A." ABC News, March 25, 2015. Retrieved November 25, 2015 (http://abcnews.go.com/Business/cfo-food-stamps-controversial-viral-video/story?id=29533695).

England, Deborah. "Cyber Avengers: White Knights or Vigilantes?" Criminal Defense Lawyer. Retrieved November 25, 2015 (http://www.criminaldefenselawyer.com/resources/cyber-avengers-white-knights-or-vigilantes.htm).

Hansen, Kevin A. "Seven Shocking Bully Regrets." Huffington Post, June 22, 2012. Retrieved November 25, 2015 (http://www.huffingtonpost.com/kevin-a-hansen/bullying_b_1617570.html).

Klonick, Kate. "Re-Shaming the Debate: Social Norms, Shame, and Regulation in an Internet Age." *Maryland Law Review*, August 1, 2015. Retrieved November 25, 2015 (http://ssrn.com/abstract=2638693 or http://dx.doi.org/10.2139/ssrn.2638693).

Lala, Elisa. "Father's Viral Video Sparks Conversation on Cyber Shaming Kids." *Philly Voice*, June 2, 2015. Retrieved November 25, 2015 (http://www.phillyvoice.com/parents-video-sparks-convo-against-shaming-kids).

Lewinsky, Monica. "The Price of Shame." Ted Talk, March 2015. Retrieved November 22, 2015 (https://www.ted.com/talks/monica_lewinsky_the_price_of_shame?language=en).

Mackinley, Paige. "Justine Bieber: Gay Is 'Not an Insult' in Response to Internet Gay Shaming." Inquisitr.com, June 1, 2015. Retrieved November 25, 2015 (http://www.inquisitr.com/2135248/justin-bieber-i-m-not-gay-insult-kiss-male-friend-instagram-video-shaming).

Miller, Brian. "Cybershaming: 'Only Creepy People Check Past the Second Page.'" *Seattle Weekly* News, March 24, 2015. Retrieved 25, 2015 (http://www.seattleweekly.com/home/957463-129

/cybershaming-only-creepy-people-check-past).
Parents World. "Does Cyber-shaming Your Children Work?" Jan.-Feb. 2015. Retrieved November 25, 2015 (http://www.parentsworld.com.sg/does-cyber-shaming-your-children-work).
Phillips, Whitney, and Kate Miltner. "The Internet's Vigilante Shame Army." TheAwl.com, December 19, 2012. Retrieved November 25, 2015 (http://www.theawl.com/2012/12/the-internets-vigilante-shame-army).
Pitts, Byron. "Gay Student's Death Highlights Troubling Trend." CBS News, September 20, 2010. Retrieved November 25, 2015 (http://www.cbsnews.com/news/gay-students-death-highlights-troubling-trend).
Ronson, Jon. *So You've Been Publicly Shamed*. New York, NY: Riverhead Books, 2015.
Ronson, Jon. "How One Stupid Tweet Blew Up Justine Sacco's Life." New York Times Magazine, February 12, 2015. Retrieved November 25, 2015 (http://www.nytimes.com/2015/02/15/magazine/how-one-stupid-tweet-ruined-justine-saccos-life.html?_r=0).
Singel, Jesse. "Jon Ronson on Monica Lewinsky and Cybershaming." NYMag.com, March 26, 2015. Retrieved November 25, 2015 (http://nymag.com/scienceofus/2015/03/jon-ronson-on-monica-lewinsky-and-cybershaming.html).
Smith, Tovia. "Companies 'Named And Shamed' For Bad Behavior." NPR.org, March 7, 2010. Retrieved November 25, 2015 (http://www.npr.org/templates/story/story.php?storyId=124357844).

Stone, Polly Jenna. "Why Internet Vigilantism Is Dangerous." Group Think, October 23, 2013. Retrieved November 25, 2015 (http://groupthink.kinja.com/why-internet-vigilantism-is-dangerous-1450646463).

Tanenbaum, Leora. "The Truth About Slut-Shaming." Huffington Post, April 15, 2015. Retrieved November 25, 2015 (http://www.huffingtonpost.com/leora-tanenbaum/the-truth-about-slut-shaming_b_7054162.html).

Tanenbaum, Leora. *I Am Not a Slut: Slut-Shaming in the Age of the Internet.* New York, NY: Harper Perennial. 2015.

Waterflow, Lucy. "'I Lost My Job, My Reputation and I'm not Able to Date Anymore': Former PR Worker Reveals How She Destroyed Her Life One Year After Sending 'Racist' Tweet Before Trip to Africa." *Daily Mail Online*, February 16, 2015. Retrieved November 25, 2015 (http://www.dailymail.co.uk/femail/article-2955322/Justine-Sacco-reveals-destroyed-life-racist-tweet-trip-Africa.html).

INDEX

About the Author

Tracy Brown Hamilton has written many books for young adults on a variety of topics. She lives in the Netherlands with her husband and three children.

Photo Credits

Cover Stuart Jenner/Shutterstock.com; p. 5 Monkey Business Images/ Shutterstock.com; p. 8 Cindy Ord/Getty Images; p. 9 Anatoly Tiplyashin/ Shutterstock.com; p. 12 Gilbert Carrasquillo/Getty Images; p. 16 © Pat Canova/Alamy Stock Photo; p. 18 Emmanuel Dunand/AFP/Getty Images; p. 20 SolStock/E+/Getty Images; p. 23 Steve Debenport/E+/GettyImages; p. 27 Jason Hetherington/The Image Bank/Getty Images; p. 28 pixinoo/ Shutterstock.com; p. 32 H. Armstrong Roberts/Retrofile/Getty Images; p. 33 Rido/Shutterstock.com; p. 35 antoniodiaz/Shutterstock.com; p. 38 Jekaterina Nikitina/Stone/Getty Images; p. 39 Sara Press/Photolibrary/Getty Images; p. 43 Erik Von Weber/The Image Bank/Getty Images; p. 46 Bloom Productions/ Taxi/Getty Images; p. 49 tab62/shutterstock.com; cover and interior pages camouflage pattern Lorelyn Medina/Shutterstock.com; cover and interior pages texture patterns Chantal de Bruijne/Shutterstock.com, foxie/ Shutterstock.com.

Designer: Nicole Russo; Editor: Christine Poolos;
Photo Researcher: Carina Finn